D1199057

Bessie Coleman

Published in the United States of America by Cherry Lake Publishing
Ann Arbor, Michigan
www.cherrylakepublishing.com

Reading Adviser: Marla Conn, MS, Ed, Literacy Specialist, Read-Ability, Inc.
Book Designer: Jennifer Wahi
Illustrator: Jeff Bane

Photo Credits: © Joseph Sohm/Shutterstock.com, 5; © Oklahoma Historical Society/ 18827.522, Albertype Collection, 7; © Roy Harris / Shutterstock.com, 9; © Keith Tarrier, 11; © Smithsonian Institution/ID # 99-15416, 13, 22; © Library of Congress/Reproduction No. LC-DIG-ppmsca-53157/ Cline, Walter M. [1921], 15; ©The New York Public Library Digital Collections/Image ID 1169913, 1169912 /Taitt, John [1925], 17, 19, 23; © neftali / Shutterstock.com, 21; Cover, 1, 12, 14, 18, Jeff Bane; Various frames throughout, ©Shutterstock Images

Library of Congress Cataloging-in-Publication Data

Names: Spiller, Sara, author. | Bane, Jeff, 1957- illustrator.
Title: Bessie Coleman / by Sara Spiller; [illustrator] Jeff Bane.
Description: Ann Arbor, Michigan : Cherry Lake Publishing, 2019. | Series: My itty-bitty bio | Includes bibliographical references and index. | Audience: K to Grade 3.
Identifiers: LCCN 2018034505| ISBN 9781534142664 (hardcover) | ISBN 9781534140424 (pdf) | ISBN 9781534139220 (pbk.) | ISBN 9781534141629 (hosted ebook)
Subjects: LCSH: Coleman, Bessie, 1896-1926--Juvenile literature. | African American women air pilots--Biography--Juvenile literature. | Air pilots--United States--Biography--Juvenile literature.
Classification: LCC TL540.C546 S65 2019 | DDC 629.13092 [B] --dc23
LC record available at https://lccn.loc.gov/2018034505

Printed in the United States of America
Corporate Graphics

About the author: Sara Spiller is a native of the state of Michigan. She enjoys reading comic books and hanging out with her cats.

About the illustrator: Jeff Bane and his two business partners own a studio along the American River in Folsom, California, home of the 1849 Gold Rush. When Jeff's not sketching or illustrating for clients, he's either swimming or kayaking in the river to relax.

I was born in Texas. It was 1892.
I had 12 brothers and sisters.
We were poor.

I went to **college** in Oklahoma. I had to pay. But I ran out of money. I moved to Chicago.

Do you think people should pay for school? Why or why not?

I worked in a **barbershop**.

There was a war. I heard stories about **pilots** in the war.

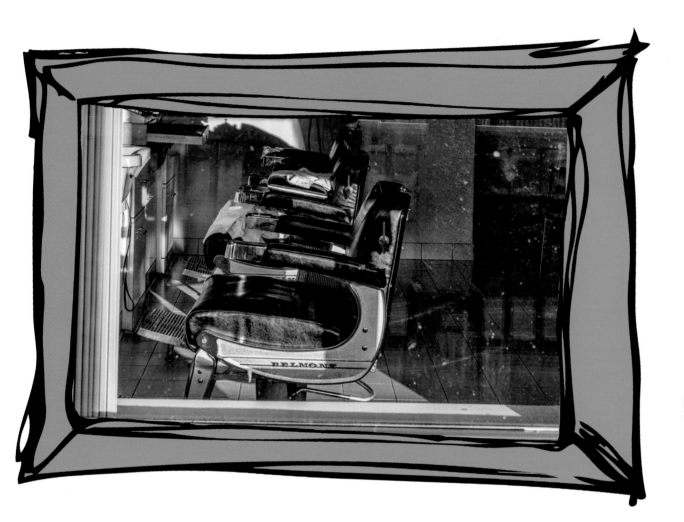

I wanted to be a pilot. I wanted to fly planes. I needed to go to flight school. But no U.S. school wanted me. They didn't want black students.

I taught myself French. I went to France.

French schools taught black students. I learned to fly a plane in France.

What language would you teach yourself?

I returned to the United States.

I performed tricks in the air.
I **barnstormed**. I **parachuted** out of my plane!

I wanted to open a flight school for black people. This school would help them become pilots. This type of school would be the first in the United States.

Who would you like to help?

I traveled. I gave talks to black people. I did air shows. I wanted blacks at my shows to be treated fairly.

I died in an **accident**. I was 34.

But I made history. I was the first black pilot in the United States.

What would you like to ask me?

1919

1890

Born
1892

Died
1926

1922

1990

glossary

accident (AK-sih-duhnt) an unlucky and unplanned event

barbershop (BAHR-bur-shahp) a place where men get their hair cut

barnstormed (BAHRN-stormd) performed tricks in the air

college (KAH-lij) a school where students can continue to study after finishing high school

parachuted (PA-ruh-shoot-ed) used a large piece of strong but light fabric to slow a fall from a plane

pilots (PYE-luhts) people who fly planes

index